Swarthmore Lectur

REASONABLE UNCERTAINTY

a Quaker approach to doctrine

by Gerald Priestland

QUAKER HOME SERVICE · LONDON

First published July 1982

© Gerald Priestland 1982

ISBN 0 85245 161 X

Cover design by John Blamires

*Printed in Great Britain in 11/12 Photon
Times by Headley Brothers Ltd., The
Invicta Press, Ashford, Kent and London*

PREFACE

The Swarthmore Lectureship was
established by the Woodbrooke Extension
Committee at a meeting held December 9th,
1907: the minute of the Committee
providing for 'an annual lecture on some
subject relating to the message and work of
the Society of Friends'. The name
Swarthmore was chosen in memory of the
home of Margaret Fox, which was always
open to the earnest seeker after Truth, and
from which loving words of sympathy and
substantial material help were sent to fellow
workers.

The lectureship has a twofold purpose: first,
to interpret further to the members of the
Society of Friends their message and
mission; and, secondly, to bring before the
public the spirit, the aims and fundamental
principles of Friends. The lecturer alone is
responsible for any opinions expressed.

The lectureship provides both for the
publication of a book and for the delivery of a
lecture, the latter usually at the time of
assembly of London Yearly Meeting of the
Society of Friends. A lecture related to the
present book was delivered in the Arts Centre
Hall, University of Warwick, on the evening of
Sunday, 25th July, 1982.

INTRODUCTION

The theme of this lecture is as follows:

According to the Queries,[1] Friends have declared themselves to be within the worldwide Christian Church. Yet they mostly abstain from the doctrines that define that Church. How alien are such doctrines to the spirit of Quakerism? Should Friends take more interest in them, or would that risk be betraying our traditions?

Accustomed as I am to public speaking, I have faced no audience more terrifying—more truly calculated to make me quake—than one composed of Friends. The sternest reviews of the books I have written have usually been in *The Friend*—and this is right and proper. There is no place in the Society of Friends for Men of the Year or cults of personality: for the one thing that prevents what could so easily become a bundle of private religions from going mad is the exposure of ministry to rigorous (though, one hopes, prayerful and charitable) examination by the meeting: if need be, by the Society as a whole.

Which is a way of apologising for what cannot for long be concealed, that this lecture arises out of a series of broadcasts entitled *Priestland's Progress*[2] which was broadcast over BBC Radio 4 during the autumn of 1981. Written and compiled by myself and produced by my colleague Chris Rees, it sought to explore (for the enlightenment of a lay audience increasingly deprived of religious instruction) some of the basic doctrines of mainstream Christianity. Among these were the Authority of Scripture, Sin, Salvation, the Trinity, Worship and Prayer, Sacraments, the Church.

Few of these have much currency among Friends, which was one reason why Friends were barely represented among the 102

1

witnesses interviewed for the series. But that was not the only reason, and I should like to take this opportunity to give some others.

For a start, even with ten hours of broadcasting at our disposal it was necessary to narrow the field down if the result was not to be a wild confusion of sectarian arguments. With due respect for those who would maintain that Quakerism *is* the true mainstream of Christianity, one can only record that numerically it has failed to demonstrate that it is. And if one had granted more time to Quaker heterodoxy, one could not have denied equal time to the Mormons, Unitarians, Seventh Day Adventists and many others. The object was, however, not to display a competitive bazaar of faiths but to say 'These are the teachings that underlie *most* of the churches. Start from here, think for yourself and make your own pilgrimage of faith.' One further point: since the narrator was himself a Quaker, and declared himself to be, the Society and its tendencies were not wholly unrepresented. Indeed, there were some listeners (not many, I am glad to say) who suspected a Quaker bias throughout.

Aware of the danger, I will admit that I leant over backwards *not* to press Quaker interpretations, with the result that I received a number of letters saying 'You have told us what the Church thinks on these matters, but what do *you* think?' What canst *thou* say? It would have been improper for me to use the broadcasts as a free platform for my personal theology; but I take it that this lecture can be precisely that, and I shall use it as such. Now that I am no longer a staff correspondent of the BBC the restraints of impartiality are loosened, though never, I hope, the duty to be reasonable and fair. Nor should I ever wish it to be thought that working for that admirable Corporation had placed me under any kind of duress. I am profoundly grateful for the opportunities and freedom of thought it has afforded me.

And so, in what follows, I wish to retrace some of my steps on that *Progress,* to look more deeply into my own reactions to what I learnt, and to face—as a Christian as well as a Quaker—the implications for my Quakerism of Christian doctrine as I see it. Let it never be said that I am trying to foist dogma upon the Society of Friends. But let it never be said, either, that having spent some months among doctrinal Christians I have dodged the question 'What canst *thou* say?'

1

The proposition from which I take my title is that the Christian Faith is not—as many outsiders take it to be—a system of unreasonable certainties, but one of reasonable uncertainties. By uncertainties I do not mean doubts, and by reasonable I do not mean logical. What I am talking about are beliefs—even convictions—that cannot be proved symbolically, like chemical or mathematical processes, yet which have a consistency which does not discredit the believer. As articulated by the believer they are clearly not the whole story—they are open-ended and liable to emendation or development; but the believer may claim of them that they check with experience—which others may confirm—and that above all, they make sense of life and make sense in life.

What I have said there already raises several questions: above all, about the meaning of 'making sense'. And whatever it is, am I saying that a system is admirable simply because it makes sense in its own terms—is self-confirming? It should not be too difficult to devise several systems that do that; including, paradoxically, the atheist view that there is no sense in life at all and that the Universe is fundamentally absurd—that it is, literally, deaf and has nothing to answer back to us. No, consistency is not enough. I would say that absolute consistency is too much—for it leaves no room for the mystery which I still find in spite of my beliefs; and I expect to encounter mysteries because (believing in God as I do) I do not expect His ways to be exactly like mine, or my mind to be capable of understanding more than a small corner of His. But perhaps I am cheating by playing the 'God' card so soon in the game.

I think the best approach to the meaning of 'making sense' lies through the phenomenon of experience: and here, I believe, we have the very door to Quakerism. You will, I am sure, excuse me if I quote, yet again, that passage from George Fox's *Journal* which was for me—and has been for so many—the opening of the spiritual vision:

> And when all my hopes in them and in all men were gone, so that I had nothing outwardly to help me, nor could tell what to do, then, Oh then, I heard a voice which said, 'There is one, even Christ Jesus, that can speak to thy condition', and when I heard it my heart did leap for joy. Then the Lord did let me see why there was none upon the earth that could speak to my condition, namely, that I might give Him all the glory; for all are concluded under sin, and shut up in unbelief as I had been, that Jesus Christ might have the pre-eminence, who enlightens, and gives grace, and faith, and power. Thus, when God doth work who shall let it? And this I knew experimentally.[3]

Those last words are of the essence: experimentally—by experience, by his own personal experience within. Fox has already told us how the institutional priests and independent preachers had failed to make sense of life—'There was none among them all that could speak to my condition', he says; but now, when at last he has stopped listening to others and been left with nothing but his own experience, now he hears the message that makes sense. And modern Quakers may have to admit that it is much less sophisticated—much more like a poster outside an evangelical tin chapel—than we might fancy. Jesus Christ enlightens, gives grace and faith and power. In fact, JESUS SAVES.

What happens next is a splendid demonstration of what 'making sense' means. Fox has realised why it was that all his

6

previous attempts to understand life had come to nothing. Christ had wanted him to go directly to the source, not to drink from gutters that were already tainted. That made sense of the past. But it is a quality of the truth that it makes sense not only of the past—giving it a purpose—but that we can use it to lead us purposefully forward, finding more and more things that fit into the pattern, that are right and proper in their place. Fox keeps saying that Christ 'opened' things to him—the Scriptures, the true natures of the people he met, the very heart of human sin and human goodness. And he died saying he was 'fully clear'. It all made sense to him.

Now, I am no Foxian scholar. I have said elsewhere that I found him a real deterrent to joining the Society of Friends. This was not just because of his apparent humourlessness, arrogance and vindictiveness, but because I find much of his writing very hard to understand: and I do not see how one can understand it unless one knows much more than I do about the theological currency of seventeenth-century England. Some of us like to think that Fox simply read the New Testament and was inspired to recreate a primitive do-it-yourself Christianity. Certainly he knew the gospels very well—he knew the entire Bible much better than most of us today; and certainly he thought he was taking his followers back to the original church of the apostles, as most reformers do. But I think he had read and heard more continental theology (and been influenced by it) than appears on the surface of that woodcut prose of his. And although he was immune to the mediaeval accretions of the Catholic Church, he could not have been unaffected—as a Bible-reading man—by the extremely subtle theology of St. Paul, and the other epistle-writers. The whole imagery of the Light and the Seed goes back to them.

What I have been working towards is this: that there never was a time, even among Friends, when the religious way of 'making sense' did not involve the taking in of certain doctrines. Friends like to think that they have never imposed tests of belief upon each other (though I am not so sure) and certainly, today, we are extremely tolerant—to the point where a newcomer in our midst finds it hard to make out *what* we believe, if anything. One gets the impression that the average Quaker meeting consists half of people who are resting (perhaps permanently) from the doctrinal battlefield, and half of people who have smuggled in their own favourite doctrines from other churches and are quietly picnicking off them in the Meeting House—for there is little to be found in the meeting's own larder.

No doubt you have heard all this before. It has been a recurring theme of Swarthmore Lectures. As recently as 1980, Janet Scott spoke 'towards a Quaker Theology',[4] which came to its climax in a dazzling (and in some ways blinding) awareness of the creative God. Earlier, in 1965, the great but under-estimated John Macmurray[5] urged us towards an 'undogmatic, hypothetical and temporary' theology which would recognise that 'it is impossible to believe what one does not understand, and undesirable to profess to believe what one cannot believe effectively'. I have to say I do not find those last remarks altogether satisfactory: I do not know what 'believing effectively' means, but I do know that I believe things I don't understand fully. I believe in the goodness of God, for example: but I should be very suspicious of myself if I claimed to understand it.

I indulged in that little pirouette for a purpose: namely that of showing that you cannot open the door to theology—words about God, literally—without admitting something that may seem alien to the whole spirit of Quakerism—namely, disunity. The silence, we are told, brings unity: for that is where we are gathered into God and He is our sole expression. A great soul of the Russian Orthodox Church once told me that, to him, sin was superficiality—the refusal to go deep into our beings, where God

8

lay and where there could be no conflict between individuals, because we were all at one there.

This is all very well. It is very well indeed. Such a unity with God and each other lies at the very heart of any Quaker meeting that really works. But we cannot sit in silence, with ourselves, with other Friends or with the rest of the world forever. We have to discuss and even argue. For it is in the nature of humanity to endeavour to press forward. More particularly, Friends are not and never have been a purely contemplative sect. In some ways, that is odd. At first sight, you might have thought it inevitable that we should become a people set apart in private communities—like the Shakers—but we have not done so. We have engaged in industry and commerce, and today, more than ever, we are fully integrated into secular society and (one hopes) in conversation with it. We like to think that we preach by example rather than by precept; but if we make any impact at all with the former, people are bound to ask us about the latter, and I do not think it is enough to tell them just to be still and listen. That is a great treasure, to be sure; but I doubt if it can be uncovered by an enquirer who comes to the search without charts, tools or provisions of any kind. Can we supply them? Have we anything to compete with the secular kits offered by science, politics, economics or the many schools of mind-manipulating pseudo-religion? There will always, I think, be natural Quakers who make their way into the Society of Friends in the last stages of their spiritual pilgrimage—perhaps I am one myself. But it is not worthy of us to become a spiritual geriatric home. Fox never saw us like that—he actually believed we were, or would become, the one Great Church, and though I don't think that was ever likely, I do not think, either, that we have raised our lamp high enough for all to see.

I must be personal here, in order to be honest; though, for those who know these things already, I shall be brief. I came to the Society by way of the Church of England and the English Presbyterian Church: therefore, while I would say that I owe those churches such religious instruction as I already have, you may say I have been biased by my upbringing towards a doctrinaire Christianity. I am also a journalist: therefore while I may express my disappointment at the Society's lack of enthusiasm for publicity, you may say that I fail to appreciate your reservations about the blessings of the mass media. Let us keep all those things charitably in mind as we continue. I, for one, am humbly aware of being privileged at this moment, but I do not think that confers upon me any magical power to persuade you against your will.

As an ecumenical Quaker, that is, one who takes seriously the claim of Query 23[5] that we are 'within the world-wide Christian church' and should 'try to share in the life and fellowship of the whole Christian community' I take a special view of doctrine and theology which is contingent upon our relationship with that church. I am not arguing that we should become a doctrinal community ourselves, in the way that most others are: I still believe that we have a unique contribution to make to the wider religious community by continuing to be ourselves and by continuing to do our own thing. But I also believe that we cannot make that contribution as fully as we should—as fully as we are called on to do by Christ—unless we understand what the others are up to and do indeed share in that fellowship and life.

For if we are not to become the whole Church ourselves (and with a remarkably stable membership over the past century and more, how should we?) and if we are not to merge into some other denomination (and with our tradition, how could we?) then it seems to me that we must accept our role as a kind of lay order within the existing Great Church: a quiet chapel in the great cathedral, contributing our eloquent silence to the mass.

10

No: I am not calling upon the Society to endorse the Covenant for Church Unity and send up the Clerk of Yearly Meeting to be ordained—apostolically or otherwise—as a bishop. Fox forbid such a thing! In any case, I should be appalled to find we were even eligible. It is very important, in my view, that the churches be told that we regard ourselves as part of them even if we don't pass their tests. As a matter of fact, I only met one clergyman in all my Progress (and he a foreigner) who denied that we were. It is right and proper that we should be an experimental branch of the Church—in the scientific, post-Foxian sense of 'experiment'. We have a freedom to open our minds to new light, from whatever quarter it may arise, which they inevitably find alarming. But it is part of my purpose now, in discussing the Reasonable Uncertainty of the Christian Faith, to argue that we shall be departing from our mission if we become no more than a loose association of groups engaged in metaphysical speculation, detached from our Christian roots and indifferent to the mainstream of Christian thought. I *hope* that the mainstream needs us. I am quite sure that we need it.

2

You will often hear it said that Friends subscribe to no doctrine at all; or at least, to no dogma—which, in its secondary usage, has a more derogatory sense. But you have only to consult our anthology *Christian Faith and Practice*[7] to realise that this is hardly so.

There you will find William Dewsbury (dated 1656) witnessing to Christ 'who was born of the Virgin, suffered at Jerusalem, and rose again the third day, and ascended into Heaven, and sitteth at the right hand of God . . .' There, too, you will find William Penn insisting that Quakers do believe in 'the Holy Three, and that these Three are truly and properly One', though he adds that Friends prefer the scriptural terms and are reluctant to adopt the language of theologians 'from whence people are apt to entertain gross ideas and notions'. I must say, I wonder how anyone who claimed to be speaking the language of scripture could affirm himself a trinitarian.

Perhaps we should hurry on to the next entry in *Christian Faith and Practice,* where we find Isaac Penington also declaring his Trinitarianism and citing both the First Epistle of John and (more soundly, perhaps, from a Quaker point of view) his own 'experimental knowledge': 'For I know three and feel three in spirit, even an Eternal Father, Son and Holy Spirit, which are but one eternal God.'

I suspect that many Friends today would be embarrassed to hear such language at meeting. As they might be to hear that of Yearly Meeting in 1879, evangelically proclaiming 'The Lord Jesus is the propitiation for our sins'. I wonder how many Friends today believe in Propitiation; or even (as the footnote offers it) Expiation? Are modern Friends even united with Fox himself in believing that the scriptures were 'given forth by the Holy Spirit of God' and are 'the words of God'?

Again, I am not trying to nudge the Society into becoming a rather low branch of the Church of England. What I am trying to do is to illustrate how, not so very long ago, we shared far more of the common language of the churches than we do today. Perhaps I should say 'more than we appear to share today'; for I suspect that a majority of Friends are more old-fashioned in their Christianity than the articulate minority featured in the columns of *The Friend*. It is also true that, since the beginning, Friends have qualified their adherence to doctrine in ways that would not have been acceptable to the institutional churches. Fox, for example, believed in sin: but he also believed that he had been freed from sin—which remains a great heresy in the eyes of the Church. And no evangelical can be happy with the persistent claim of Friends that, to quote Yorkshire Quarterly Meeting in 1919, 'The canon of Scripture may be closed, but the inspiration has not ceased ... The life comes to us not from the record itself but from communion with Him of whom the record tells'.[8]

Nervousness at that kind of claim comes from a fear of indiscipline. Goodness knows what wild prophecies may break out if people are allowed to go further than the printed word of scripture, claiming as their authority a direct communion with God! You and I know what happens, of course. In my experience, at any rate, wildness is all too rare among Friends; and if there were any, it would either be ignored or be cooled down by the icy breath of weighty elders. Of all the religious groups in this country, Quakers are the least likely to publish radical religious ideas, partly because (as I have said) so many Friends have come to the Society to seek refuge from theological argument.

One cannot but respect that. It is a weakness of the other

churches that so few of them offer their members anything beyond the busy-ness of liturgical worship, argumentative teaching, vocal expression and social activity. Some of them know this: the Catholics, in particular, do understand that silence is the very heart of prayer; and Anglican services nowadays are punctuated with the rubric 'Here silence may be kept'—though, alas, it seldom is, or not for long.

So our ways are not without echoes in other churches, and the same is true of our philosophy. One of the things that surprised me in my pilgrimage among the church thinkers of this country was the extent to which so many agreed with the spirit of that Yorkshire epistle which I quoted, that the inspiration of the Holy Spirit has not ceased, and that the light and life and truth come to us not from the dry record but our meeting with God within it.

Some of you will say: 'But you have been lucky. By chance or deliberately, you have been talking to progressive theologians like Hans Küng, Jurgen Moltmann, Maurice Wiles and Dennis Nineham. They are very different from the stuffy priests and bishops we know. To them, the Pope is literally right or the Bible is literally true and that's that!'

I will not deny that there is still a great deal of that about, or that the congregations and theological colleges which are booming today do tend to be un-liberal, even reactionary. That is not entirely the fault of the priesthood and ministry. Most of the main-stream churches in this country—including the Roman Catholics—have been inviting their people to participate in the conduct and development of their faith. But the reaction of many congregations has been to shrink back in terror and call for more—not less—authoritarianism, more certainty, less adventure. In some churches this has taken the form of a flight from reason into various kinds of emotional expression, Pentecostal, Charismatic, 'speaking in tongues'. I may have

15

been guilty, at times, of overemphasising the rational side of religion—it is not just head, of course, but heart and guts as well—but I do not believe that the forces of secularism and materialism can be answered with Glossolalia, or with snippets of scripture. They have to be met by the whole Christian, the whole believer, in all his aspects, but most notably—in an age that prides itself on its reason—by the reasonable, reasoning Christian, ready to do battle for his uncertainties.

Now it may sound tactless to invite Quakers to a battle, but we have fought for the truth often enough in the past, in our own way, and today I think we have two simultaneous campaigns to fight. The first is going on within the churches, and the second between the churches and the forces of secularism. Why should we join either? Why should we not sit them out and cultivate our own walled garden, hoping that the combatants will wear each other out and that when peace comes, through mutual exhaustion, we shall be left on our feet holding the banner of truth?

I cannot be sure that won't happen; but I dare not be certain that it will. It is by no means impossible that the forces of unreason will carry the churches, which will then fall to those of militant secularism. What makes us think the victors will spare the Society of Friends? It seems to me short-sighted as well as intellectually dishonest to stay out of either battle. With due respect to those Friends who cannot bring themselves to associate with the priested churches, I believe we should do what we can to support progressive Christianity both against religious reaction and against atheistic materialism.

But there are two objections I can foresee: first, from those dear Friends of mine who hesitate to call themselves Christians not because they do not revere Christ, but because of what His followers have made of the Church; and second, from those who believe it would be no bad thing if the churches were to fade away and we were to find ourselves in a secularised society

16

which spontaneously followed the way of Christ, loving God and doing good.

I cannot help sympathising with the first group of objectors—those who are allergic to the Church. At first sight, I must admit, it seems an irrelevant and often ludicrous object. I still cannot forget a photograph which appeared in the *Church Times* earlier this year, of the Archbishop of Canterbury posing with three bishops whom he had just consecrated: in all their finery, they had a Beatrix Potter look about them, like three little kittens who'd found their mittens. To imagine them ministering to a dole queue—let alone walking the hills of first century Galilee—seemed outrageous, almost impossible. And yet, knowing them as I do, I can assure you they were all good, faithful and compassionate men. It was not they, but the aura of the Church, which mocked Christ.

And yet, after my pilgrimage, it is my belief that we all need the Church, and that to pretend that Quakers are not of it does not alter the fact that we are. I shall argue this point in greater detail later; but if you attempt to distinguish between Christianity and Churchianity—to say that you are all for the Gospel and the example of Christ, but all against the Thirtynine Articles and the Westminster Confession—I would have to reply that I am sorry, but I do not see how you could have had the one without the other. The other, the Churchianity, may well need changing; indeed, it knows very well that it does, and it can be changed, it is changing, and perhaps we can help it if we join in. As for the Christianity: I suppose it is not enough to tell objectors that Fox believed Quakers were Christians—the only real Christians—and that Queries 2, 4, 5, 9 and 23[9] make it perfectly clear that we still are. And if people like Ninian Smart and John Robinson can put an arm around Buddhism or Hinduism and still call themselves Christians, why should an exploring Quaker feel obliged to deny the title? Doubts, to the extent of negative convictions, about the divinity of Christ are as common in the churches today as doubts about the Virgin Birth. Hierarchies growl 'Heresy!' but in fact the caravan goes on its way.

If the objections I have mentioned to being included in the Church are conscientious ones, the theory that the death of the churches might be no bad thing is a matter of practical speculation (supposing there is such a thing). There is, apparently, a movement among the protestant churches in this country to hold a great congress in 1984. Orwell's prophecies must have something to do with the choice of year, but those who are behind the congress evidently feel a movement of the Spirit towards such a gathering, and I think they are right. There has been much thrashing about in recent years over the organisational details of Church Unity, and much shuffling of definitions among Anglican and Roman Catholic theologians, but very little attention to where the spiritual wind is actually blowing.

The Church—any church—is called on by God to be creative: to join Him in the continuous process of creations; and among creative organisations these days there is a technique which I think such a congress might find useful. I have seen it used by broadcasting producers to find ideas for programmes, and it consists of taking seriously the notions one would normally suppress—because they are too way-out, taboo, contradictory of all accepted principles. This is not to say they are necessarily to be adopted (though it is surprising how many of them can be, with success): it is the discussion of them that leads to such useful discoveries.

I submit that if there is a 1984 congress, it should seriously consider the proposition that the churches should abolish themselves: disband, sell up, shut down. Let me say at once that I am quite certain they would speedily re-form in different shapes. But whether it happened or was only talked about, the process

18

would oblige people to think seriously about what the Church means to them, why they need it, and what they need.

I think we need the Church for three main reasons. Above all, we need it to keep alive the stories about God. I am aware that this emphasis on 'story' is a current vogue among theologians, but I believe it is with good cause—one that should appeal to Friends. We need the Society of Friends to keep alive the stories about Quakers, about George Fox and the Valiant Sixty, about William Penn, about our seventeenth-century martyrs, about Elizabeth Fry, about countless witnesses who not only talked and prayed Quakerism but did and lived Quakerism. That, I believe, is the secret of our unlikely survival; and I do not think those stories would have been kept alive and in circulation without the institutional society, collecting, publishing, circulating and preserving those stories.

It is so, on a larger scale, with other churches and with Christianity itself—and before it, with Judaism. It is so with every other religion. There is always some sort of organisation, some tradition of scholarship and publication, which guards and publishes the scriptures. And at the heart of those scriptures is the story—the story of Vishnu, Buddha, Moses, Jesus, Muhammed and their saints.

You may say 'But these can be handed on in popular tradition; or, nowadays, be printed by anybody. We don't need a self-serving priesthood to vet them!' It is not so simple. Stories, even when they are down on paper, are fragile, destructible, easily perverted. Any journalist or historian knows how quickly a story can break up into several different versions: somebody has to decide which is the right one, or at least (as in the case of the New Testament) which of many gospels deserve respect. Translation involves responsibility. There are some oddly slanted versions of the Bible in circulation today, but, by and large, we do best to place our confidence in those authorised by

19

the oldest churches.

It is the stories about God, rather than the doctrines derived from them, that are central to the Christian Faith. I acknowledge that the Bible is not just a story-book and that the gospel stories have often been selected to illustrate doctrine. From this I draw three conclusions: that Jesus Himself taught doctrine; that even Friends must be aware of doctrine; and that, nevertheless, the stories still stand behind it all, creative, human and open-ended—leading on. I do not think we could have them without the Church teaching, preaching and celebrating them.

We need the Church secondly for discipline and authority. This may shock some Friends, for surely the very origin of Quakerism lay in resisting any such impositions?

You may have noticed that I have not yet defined what I mean by 'the Church', though I have sometimes contrasted it with 'the churches'. The very fact that I have been able to do so indicates that it is a word we do instinctively—if vaguely—understand. It is the community of all who claim to follow Christ (that above all) and any attempt to exclude some followers and claim precedence for others must be subservient to this. It is the whole people of Christ, not just the priesthood (which is good Catholic theology, by the way) and it seems to me that Quakers are a part of it in that sense and would not wish to be otherwise.

Because it is a human community, the Church cannot help organising itself: that is what humans invariably do, and organisation invariably involves pressure to conform. Sometimes it is coercive and sometimes it is persuasive, and it is a measure of maturity how much persuasion and how little coercion an organisation can exercise and still remain a recognisable whole. The Society of Friends likes to think it relies upon the persuasion of the Spirit for its unity, and I am sure that is in us; but it would be a naive Friend who did not occasionally

20

sense other, more human, pressures in the Society. There *is* a discipline and authority among Quakers, and I think the simplest way to describe it is Tradition.

I suppose the Roman Catholic Church, and certainly the Orthodox, would say the same, although their traditions are more formally codified and policed, and I would certainly defend the assertion of discipline by the Church in some form. Outsiders often imagine that a meeting for worship is a collection of individual meditations, and that Quakers make up their own personal religions. We know it is not like that at all: that a meeting is wandering and impoverished if it is not drawing upon what has been handed down to us, and that its worship is a failure if the individuals attempting it are not gathered into unity.

Religion that is purely private and personal is, to me, a sorry thing. Let me make myself clear: there must be a direct personal apprehension of the divine at the heart of any living faith—the 'experimental knowledge' of the original Friends. The way of the mystic, the seeker, is mine also. But those early seekers were never solitaries. They shared their insights, so that those who were gifted could encourage and enlighten those who were not, and those who were carried away by foolish or dangerous delusions could be corrected by wiser spirits.

Private religion is sometimes very shallow. People make the amazing discovery that God Loves Us, or that We Ought to Love One Another, and then hug that to them and go no further. Private religion is sometimes very selfish, leading to the conclusion that the people next door are damned and I am saved, so I should have nothing to do with them. And, at its worst, private religion can go mad, urging us to spit on Jews or kill prostitutes. There have been cases where the sharing of such madness, far from bringing correction, has made converts. There is no safety to be promised in small numbers. This, it seems to me, strengthens the case for a wider church drawing

21

upon tried and tested traditions.

The third reason for needing the Church follows from the second. We need the Church to remind us that a faith—particularly the Christian faith—is a community. Spiritually and intellectually its followers enrich, correct and support one another; but we are also enjoined to love one another, to be a society of friends. Jesus makes it very clear, in stories like that of the Good Samaritan, that loving one another means caring for one another even if we do not particularly *like* one another. You do not have to be *in love* with your neighbour in order to exercise your Christian duty towards him.

It would be wrong to imagine that our caring can be confined to members of our own church: that was another meaning of the Good Samaritan. But belonging to a church—and to *the* Church—does remind us constantly that we may not limit our care to ourselves and our blood relations: that we belong to a wider family. It is my argument that just as the individual Christian should accept his membership of a congregation, so Quakers should accept their membership of the Christian Church: and, to go further, that the Christian Church should accept its membership of the wider family of faiths.

3

So I believe that we, as Quakers, need the Church and need to recognise and demonstrate that we are part of it. In practical terms I should like to see us making ourselves heard and felt unmistakeably in the British Council of Churches, the World Council, the theological community, the church pulpit, and the religious press and broadcasting. (I know there are credal difficulties in the World Council; but that does not prevent Jean Zaru from playing an extremely effective role on the Central Committee.) At a humbler level, I would like to see more Friends attending services at their local churches and making themselves known there. Often—though not, I am afraid, always—they would find the experience enriched their return to meeting; and I do know of Friends who value deeply their occasional taking of Holy Communion. I see nothing to deplore in that.

But what about those creeds—those doctrines?

I will let you into a secret, which has, in fact, been wide open for years past to anyone who cared to peep. Church Christianity is not a *table d'hôte* menu. It is *à la carte*. You are not obliged to swallow what you do not wish to swallow. You may, indeed, hear things in church with which you do not agree, but nobody will burn you at the stake for disagreeing with them, and I should be very surprised if they even showed you the door.

I can imagine two kinds of reaction to that sort of talk. One goes: 'But you are advocating intellectual dishonesty—or at least asking us to sit through a load of meaningless mumbo-jumbo'. To which I reply that, on the contrary, I am advocating the intellectual honesty to examine other people's traditions and try to ascertain what they mean; and the humility to grant that other Christians are not necessarily idiots.

The other reaction—less likely to come from Friends, perhaps, than church-people—is that I am encouraging a shop-as-you-please Christianity, with no other standard than personal taste. Well, like the Catholics, I believe in the supremacy of conscience; but like them, too, I insist that it has to be an informed conscience. That is half the point of knowing about doctrine, to be informed about the thinking and teaching on a given subject and to share in the discoveries of a rich treasury of minds, not a few of them better than our own. Of course it will not do to adopt ideas simply because they please us. They must also carry conviction that they are right and true. An idea that does not speak to our condition—that does not produce an echo from something already within us—is ineffective: it is not really part of our faith, and no amount of argument or vain repetition can make it so. Only that 'experimental knowledge' can bring it to life, and only the continuing experience of it can keep it living.

One of the ancient theologians—I think it was Augustine of Hippo—wrote that doctrine was 'only an alternative to silence'. If one insisted on speaking, this was the best one could do: it could never be the *whole* truth. Friends might have a simple response to that: then why not shut up? Why be so presumptuous as to try and set boundaries to the divine, to weigh and measure it and say 'This you must believe about it'?

Well, silence is the well of all wisdom. But I do not think it is the well that we worship, not just an empty hole. The well contains water, which we may draw out from it and use. I know there are some, in the Orient, who seek to annihilate themselves utterly into nothingness, but I do not think that is our way, it never has been. The early Quakers, by all accounts, drew a great many words out of the silence, to try to express and celebrate what they had found there, though it can never be the thing itself. The churches, I believe, are trying to do the same: to

24

express and celebrate what *they* have found, though at a rather different well.

Quakers, perhaps, are somewhat too modest in their efforts to communicate what they know about God. Modern Friends, I suspect, would rather leave it to poets, painters and composers. They are rightly shy of putting down anything which implies an obligation or compulsion to believe: they do not want to limit anyone's freedom to experience in his own terms, and least of all the Spirit's freedom to blow where it listeth.

I do not think one can deny that for centuries the churches did emphasise the compulsory nature of creeds and doctrines; though I think it is a mistake to attribute this to a lust for power or a love of beating people into conformity. I am quite sure the principal motive was a devotion to what was seen as the truth. For if you believe that you have the truth you wish to protect it against insult and perversion and to pass it on intact to future generations. That is what doctrine is really about: the secure packaging of information so that it can be transmitted. Of course, further motives become attached. Once your faith becomes identified with the state or the national culture, deviations from it become unpatriotic and subversive. And if you are still at the stage of regarding religion as a kind of magic—doing the right things for God at the right time and in the right way, in order to ensure His favour—then deviations risk calling down His punishment.

The early creeds of the Church have to be seen in this light. They were attempts to preserve the truth, as the early fathers saw it, in a form that could be handed on. The stories about God were known; indeed, by that time they were written down quite reliably. I am aware that, in the light of the discovery of certain esoteric manuscripts in the past forty years, there is a current tendency to question that reliability. But I have to say that, compared with the canonical scriptures those gnostic gospels stand upon very shaky foundations indeed.

But, given the stories, the human intelligence could not help asking: what do they mean? what is their significance for us? what should we do about them? Some of the answers given to those questions were so much at variance with majority opinion that it became necessary to lay down an orthodoxy (that is, right teaching) before the truth was drowned in confusion. One has only to think of cases like that of James Nayler to admit that even Friends have felt obliged to do this from time to time—though with less savagery than most. Certainly, a large part of the creeds is devoted to putting down the errors and heresies of the early centuries, to refuting paganism and to meeting the intellectual curiosity of the eastern Mediterranean.

The creeds still embody certain symbolic 'truths', though they no longer fit our modes and categories of thought. I sometimes wonder if St Paul would even share our notion of what a 'truth' or an 'idea' is. Paganism is not a problem for us, nor polytheism, nor are most of the heresies that bothered the Councils so much; while, on the other hand, several of the questions that divide us deeply receive little or no help from the creeds. You may consult them in vain for advice on such matters as the status of the Bible, the authority of the Church, the personality of Jesus, the cult of the Virgin, the significance of the Eucharist, the existence of the Devil and the problems of sin and suffering. Either the early Church had no doubts on these matters or they had not arisen.

When they did arise, academic doctrine was the result, and it was doctrine with a vengeance. I do not think it is frivolous to suggest that one reason for the rigour of early and mediaeval theology was that there was nothing much else for the best minds of the age to do: with the end of the Greco-Latin classical age, the Church took over virtually the whole of literacy, including philosophy, logic, natural science, politics and history. There has been a great liberation since the Renaissance, and nobody would deny that science would never have got where it is if it had remained a monopoly of the Church; but I would dare to say that the Church has now withdrawn too far, and we are left with science based upon an inadequate system of values. Doctrine is never entirely arbitrary.

In the course of my pilgrimage, I found no serious theologian in the main stream of any tradition who was prepared to say of doctrine 'This is the absolute and complete truth'. They might say 'This is true in the sense that it is not false. We believe it contains the truth, though we are not able to comprehend it fully'. They would often add 'Doctrine is provisional, it is corrigible, it is always possible that there is more than this—indeed, there must be more'. And I found this urge to strain forward, to add to our understanding of God, as lively in the Roman Catholic Church as I did among Protestants (if I may use that term, somewhat carelessly, to include Anglicans).

I did not come away feeling that the churches were dead wood incapable of bearing blossom or fruit. Their gnarled trunks may appear to stand where they always did. But their topmost branches are green and spreading in the light. I beg Friends not to flatter themselves that our little bush is the only one alive.

One of the drawbacks of Quakerism in its ultra-tolerant contemporary form is that it offers very little to push against. That, I think, is one of the most important functions of doctrine. It gives the enquirer some framework to climb in, the reformer something to challenge, the debater something to debate. In the world of Science, it is necessary to engage the established body of knowledge in dialogue, in its own language, if you want to prove your new discoveries.

To put it another way: doctrine provides the explorer of God with a set of tools and techniques with which he can tackle the mountain-face. If he declines to use them, he cuts himself off from a wealth of experience and forces himself to start from scratch. In one sense he must: for his own experience is irreplaceable. But it is arrogant to pretent that no-one has ever been your way before and that there is nothing to be learnt from them.

I am trying to tell you that the credal and doctrinal churches from which Quakers originally revolted are now churches of reasonable uncertainty, with whom we can therefore talk. But is that the whole truth? Frankly, it is not. I have found it true of men as widely spread as Billy Graham and Basil Hume, and of theologians as far apart as Dennis Nineham and John McQuarrie. I suppose I am really talking of the English-speaking world, though you must know that English theology is very far from being the most progressive in print today. It is true—Pope John Paul II notwithstanding—that almost all the major churches in this country are calling upon their laity to participate in the development of their faith. What is not true is that the laity are responding with enthusiasm. It is among the laity and some of their priests (as opposed to bishops or their equivalent) that one finds a terrified reaction, a refusal to move forward, a clinging to the coats of authoritarian father-figures. And, as if to make my own task harder, I should like to tell you now what to Quakers will sound a theological horror-story.

4

Some weeks ago, at a conference hall in London, I attended a meeting of a Roman Catholic organisation known as PRO ECCLESIA ET PONTIFICE ('For Church and Pontiff'). Everybody was extremely kind to me, and the last thing I wish to do is bite the hand that patted me.

The object of the meeting was to pass a series of resolutions to be brought to the attention of Pope John Paul, in the hope of informing him of the *true* state of English Catholic opinion, before he fell into the hands of the English hierarchy. There was a strong and steady undercurrent of distrust of the Catholic bishops, notably of Archbishop Worlock of Liverpool and of those English bishops who had joined with Anglicans in signing what are known in the trade as the ARCIC Statements—a group of rather obscure documents in which Roman and Anglican theologians claim to have mapped out a wide area of doctrinal agreement.

There were, I should say, some nine hundred traditionalists present: for the hall seats eight hundred, it was full, and there were many standing. But I counted only twenty priests (no bishops) and one of these expressed surprise to find as many as that. No-one should take the impression that this was a representative cross-section of English Catholicism, and there is solid statistical evidence (in the recent University of Surrey/Gallup Poll[10]) to support that.

The appearance and atmosphere was very similar to that of a Tory Party conference—*honi soit qui mal y pense*—and I could not help feeling that, just as at a Tory conference, if the leader had actually walked in the mutiny would instantly have been transformed into a demonstration of loyalty. But with the cat absent, the mice became tigers themselves.

'We look to our bishops to teach the truth,' proclaimed the chairman, 'But bishops are human, they are subject to pressures from militant minorities, they are tempted to be trendy. However, there is a silent majority, sometimes repelled by silly, irreverent and grotesque innovations; and we know of many who have lapsed from the faith because of them. There must be many here who are hanging on by the skin of their teeth in grief and anguish. The fullness of this hall reveals a ground-swell among ordinary lay people to restore what has gone wrong.'

And what had gone wrong was soon revealed. 'We have to fight for the Mass in Latin again! Our seminaries are turning out liturgical illiterates. Excessive use of the vernacular has turned the Church of Peter into a Tower of Babel. One wonders,' added the chair, 'how belief in the Real Presence can survive the Liturgical Revolution.'

The next speaker, a priest who is a first-generation convert, damned the new English mass as 'verbose, banal and often mis-translated. The idea of sacrifice is missing, doctrine has been watered down or omitted, and there is not enough silence. As for the so-called Youth Masses: the notion of simplifying the Mass down to the age of the children is perverse—they should be raised up to its level. There is little reference any more to Hell, to Purgatory, to prayers for the dead. Our hymns are full of heresies, the chalice is being given to the laity, and communion given standing and in the hand, instead of kneeling and on the tongue . . .'

A third speaker (a noted polemical writer) blamed the post-Vatican Two reforms for the decline in mass attendance. 'There is no renewal of the Catholic Church in this country,' he declared, 'That is a fantasy of the church beaurocracy!' And a fourth speaker argued that for Catholic bible-scholars to question that St Matthew actually wrote his own gospel was as bad as denying the Perpetual Virginity of Mary: it was a denial of the Church's authority.

The meeting moved on to questions of morality, by which it meant largely Marriage and Sex. One lady alleged that the bishops were going round spreading the word that the Pope should address himself to questions like Unemployment, Racialism and the Third World: so the meeting firmly passed a resolution calling upon him to speak out against Divorce, Contraception, Abortion and Euthanasia.

On, next, to the religious instruction of the young. Despite their centuries of experience in such matters, it is still remarkably easy to shock traditional Catholics. The biggest gasp of horror of the whole day went up when one lady described how a priest had explained the Mass to her children: comparing his robes to 'Mummy putting on her apron to do the dinner' and introducing the Consecration with the words 'And now we come to the cooking bit'. Was it my imagination, or did I detect smelling-salts in the hall? I must say, if you are trying to give some idea of how Transubstantiation *might* take place, comparing it to the transformation of flour, milk and eggs into a lovely cake isn't such a bad idea—or so it seems to me.

Ecumenism had a rough ride, too. 'The name of our game is the imitation of Christ,' thundered the next speaker, 'Did He ever do or say anything that was ecumenical?' Apparently not. 'Ecumenism and Church Unity are antithetical,' lectured another, 'The more we are ecumenical, the more we cease to be controversial. But we cannot work for Christian Unity without becoming controversial, and so ceasing to be ecumenical.' The moral being, of course, there is only one True Church.

And so the resolutions rolled forth—not one, I think, raising more than two dozen contrary votes among the nine hundred or so. To recall just a few of them:

Priests not to involve themselves in politics.

Religious instruction of the young to be confined to those
known to uphold Catholic orthodoxy.

The use of the Catechism to be mandatory in all Catholic
schools.

The Pope to consecrate England to the Blessed Mother of
God.

All restrictions to be removed on the celebration of the
Tridentine Mass.

The sacrificial nature of the priesthood to be emphasised.

False doctrines to be suppressed.

Bishops to endorse no faith but the Catholic Faith as valid.

The proceedings closed with a spirited rendering of that grand
old hymn which includes the words:

Faith of our fathers! Mary's prayers
Shall win our country back to thee;
And through the truth that comes from God
England shall then indeed be free.

You may think that by now I should alter the title of this
lecture from *Reasonable Uncertainty* to *Unreasonable
Certainty*. Nevertheless, this is only an interlude: I hope an
instructive one. I think we should try to draw from it two
lessons, the first about who was involved, the second about what
they were seeking.

Socially, there was little doubt in my mind that these were
largely upper middle class people and that the leadership even
had aristocratic connections. There were remarkably few Irish
accents to be heard, which is surprising in so large a gathering of
Catholics. It seemed to me that what we were hearing was the
voice of the recusant traditionalists who felt they had kept the
Catholic faith alive in England during the Penal Laws and who,
when the hierarchy was restored, felt they owed little to it and

treated it with suspicion. Certainly we were hearing, too, the voice of the convert who is making up for lost time by burrowing backwards into the past he never knew; and the voice of the elderly who have seen things change too fast for their comfort; but it was also the voice of those who have known authority and lost it. That is a tone which becomes familiar in every church threatened by change, and I think we should hear it as a symptom of things moving forward, not back.

What is it, then, that such people are seeking when they try to prevent their church from moving forward or, as Catholics more subtly prefer to say, from 'developing doctrine'? Obviously there is an element, which we all possess, of not wanting to lose the familiar. We know how to handle the familiar, it is full of nostalgic overtones of the golden past, it is something we love and that loves us back. Besides, it is an effort adjusting to something new: we might make fools of ourselves adjusting to it, lose status and seniority.

But it would be cynical to explain devotion to tradition only in those terms. People genuinely believe that their doctrines encapsulate the truth. The Catholic traditionalist does not believe it, however, because it is *his* doctrine and *his* truth, but the Church's; and that Church is not a modern institution made up of his contemporaries, it is an ancient continuity going back to Christ and His apostles and guaranteed by an unbroken succession of Popes and saints and martyrs. We can debate the soundness of that—personally I think it is historically dubious and of secondary value in any case—but our arguments will matter little to the Catholic, for whom belief in the continuous authority of his church is absolutely central to being a Catholic at all. What else can you be that will give you such a sense of being so right, of being confirmed by so huge a cloud of witness, of participating in something eternal and indestructible? I think, myself, it is nonsense to suppose that when we recite the Lord's

Prayer we mean by it exactly what seventeenth-century—seventh-century—first-century Christians meant. But does not the continuity give us strength? To recite Catholic doctrine can bring even more strength, because the very act of submission to it implies a sacrifice of will, a discipline, rather like assuming the strength of an army by becoming a soldier. Ours not to reason why, ours but to believe and (if necessary) die for that belief. Such an attitude has given strength and comfort to hundreds of millions. I believe Friends are perfectly right not to submit to it themselves (we have been chosen to explore another route to the summit), but if we are to speak to that of God in others it is as well to know the language they use.

Even here we have something in common—at least one tiny overlapping corner. After my visit to the PRO ECCLESIA meeting, I had a letter from a lady member who was anxious that I should understand things properly. 'As a Quaker', she wrote, 'you will appreciate how deeply Catholics felt the loss of *silence* when this distasteful new Mass was introduced. My husband and I look back longingly and lovingly on the time when we started our working day by going each morning to Mass at Westminster Cathedral—where one received the strength and guidance in the wonderful quiet which then existed—save only for the many Sanctus bells which sounded around the Cathedral at the moment of Consecration. In those days, each chapel was occupied by a priest and his server plus the lay people, and believe me, there was more affinity—the sense of belonging and sharing—than all the hand-shaking, kissing and talk of today could ever attain.' Perhaps that is something that Friends can understand, even agree with.

Very well, then, you may say. We should be politely tolerant of the goings-on in the churches (though what you have said does not suggest they are politely tolerant of each other). But that still does not prove that Quakers need either to cultivate an interest in doctrine nor the fellowship of the doctrinal churches.

Before I tempt you into the former, let me make a suggestion about the latter. It may look absurd that there should be so many adjacent faiths, each claiming to be the one true faith. But I suspect it is a formal condition of any religion (and it was once put to me by a Muslim that it was actually a work of divine providence) that each should believe itself to be, if not the only truth, at any rate the best. It is inconceivable to me that one could be—shall we say—a devout Calvinist while *knowing* that the Evangelical Anglicans next door really had the goods; or a Hindu, while believing that the truth really lay with Christianity. In fact, a Hindu would probably regard it as unthinkable to become a Christian, because his *karma* (roughly, his fate) has made him a Hindu and it would be a subversive blasphemy to go against it. We cannot deny our birth: less of a truism than meets the eye, for many of us spend a lifetime coming to terms with it. If one is born with the options open, the problem of faith actually becomes a good deal more strenuous; but for most people, doctrinal faith is something as 'given' as one's language or one's family. It may not be the only conceivable way of organising things, but because it is the traditional way it is convenient to accept it.

Does this amount to saying that one faith is as good as another? I cannot avoid the evasive response: it all depends what you mean by good, and for whom. If God has wished us to be of a single faith, He could surely have arranged it. The fact that He did not indicates to me His delicate appreciation of our varying conditions. What I am quite sure of is that He would think little of us for failing to pursue Him to the limits of our intuition, failing to develop our spiritual equipment to meet our changing environment.

5

But surely God never changes, and that is one of the axioms of faith?

I am not sure that is true, and if my doubts are well founded we should examine doctrine in a new light, regarding it (or parts of it) as possibly true, but in a temporary or qualified way.

In speaking of God (an exercise I cannot resist) I have often used the image of a vast mountain, rising into the clouds and stretching back over the horizon. There is no question of our knowing its dimensions or seeing more than a fragment of it, and what we know of it depends upon where we are standing. A friend living a mile to the east sees a valley which to me is hidden; a friend in the next county sees an entirely different face. To one observer it is bleak and forbidding; to another, it is cloaked in gentle forest. Yet it is always the same mountain. It is our standpoint that changes, as we move through space and time, though it may appear that the changes occur in the mountain.

Physical metaphors for the metaphysical reach a certain point of usefulness and then break down. God is not, in fact, a mountain.

In the Bible, we can see God Himself changing. He begins as the legendary Creator of all that is, of Adam the Man who stands for all men, Eve the Woman for all women, and the Eden that should have been for all of us. And then He becomes Yahweh, the Lord God of Abraham, Isaac and Jacob, ruthlessly exterminating all who stand in His chosen people's way: the God of Hosts mapping out battles, the God of Righteousness drawing up a contract with Israel and prescribing the minutest details of how He shall be obeyed and worshipped. From time to time, He goes off His people—or rather, they wander from His ways and are severely punished for it.

Eventually, Yahweh tires of this legalistic existence. He grows weary, it seems, of wrestling with Israel, and starts talking of peace and suffering and a mysterious kingdom which is on earth but not of it. Blasphemously, to most Jews, He purports to take on human flesh, to die, to offer Himself to the gentiles in the form of a sacrificial meal which has something to do with rescuing us from the consequences of sin. What is more (and this makes the breach with Israel complete) whereas the God of Moses was emphatically One, the God of Christendom has become mysteriously Three—while at the same time remaining emphatically One. Look now upon this picture—and on this! Somehow or other, God has certainly changed.

I began by suggesting that it was only Man who had changed his viewpoint of God; and surely the viewpoint does change, according to whether you stand in an English university, an Indian village or a Japanese city. From all three, Man sees what is recognisably a mountain. With some effort of the imagination it can even be identified as the same mountain. However, moving through time and culture, one begins to suspect that the changes that have taken place are not solely in Man—that God may be changing in response to our changes, our needs, our capacity, even to the demands we make upon Him. *Some* things about God may not change: I suspect there are truths about Him that are eternal, His creatorship, His fatherhood (or, if you prefer it, parenthood), His love. But His expression of Himself, as Mankind has understood it, has not always had the same emphasis (to say the least). The God understood by the folk-poets of Genesis is not the same as the God of Jeremiah, who is not the same as the God of St John or St Paul. There may be traces of the one in the other, but a mighty change has taken place.

It seems to me that one of the most dynamic elements in religion—particularly in the Jewish-Christian understanding of God—lies in the concept of two-way response. We would hardly have carried on believing in our God if it were just a matter of performing actions and uttering words *in the Hope* there was somebody up there. If there were no response, it would be pointless to go on.

But a developed religion is not just the magical manipulation of God, either. For one thing, He is infuriatingly hard to manipulate. There are no words or actions guaranteed to produce results. I suppose that for thousands of years men have based their rituals on the hope that there were; or at least that God's vengeance for Man's disobedience could be mitigated. Centuries of religious doctrine and discipline have been based on the fear that whole communities might be penalised for the mis-behaviour of a few individuals. And yet we have only to read the Psalms or the Book of Job to realise that, long before scientific laws of cause and effect dominated our thinking, the efficacy of religious observance was being questioned. Why did the wicked flourish? Why did the innocent and the positively righteous suffer?

God was nagged mercilessly for the answers. But such answers as came were far more subtle than 'Because you neglected to keep the Law and broke my taboos.' And something else broke into human awareness: that God was not passively waiting in his temple to be discovered by Man—He could actively take the initiative by coming to Man. He did not necessarily wait to be called upon before He responded. Often it was His call that demanded our response. We see this constantly in the Bible, and I would say that we see it again in the Reforma-tion, in the Seekers and George Fox, and (however muffled) in Vatican II—to name only some obviously ecclesiastical examples.

Religious teaching—doctrine—has to cope with a God who is not static but active: active both in natural creation and in human history. Bible-reading Christians tend to assume that Creation was a once-for-all-time activity—as if, having created the heavens, the earth and all that therein is in six days, God retired to an eternal Sabbath, leaving us to make a mess of it. I do not believe that is the Christian message. The doctrine of Creation, as I read it, involves a continuous and continuing activity in which Mankind is—and always has been—invited to share.

We see this from the start, in that earliest myth of creation, wherein Man and Woman are given dominion over every living thing, and over every tree and fruit and seed. And it is confirmed again in God's covenant with Noah. Mankind is appointed steward over God's estate, to work with Him in the continuous flow of creation. (Incidentally, it seems to me that to treat these early chapters of Genesis as if they were a literal textbook of palaeontology is to belittle their astounding insight into a much deeper level of meaning.) I would say that God's creating Man 'in His own image' implies something more: it tells us that the seed of the Incarnation—of God being involved and expressed in human flesh—was there from the start. We shall have to look further into Incarnation in due course, but it seems to me that St Paul's linking of the first and second Adam (something which George Fox brought together in his astonishing vision of Paradise) points to that conclusion.

Just as Adam stands for all men, and at his best is doing the will of God, so all men and women at their best are doing the work of creation. Thus God is active in history, incarnate in the best of our kind. I have found general agreement among theologians that God is *only* active in history through the agency of human cooperation: not through miraculous interventions that brush mankind aside. His natural order may present us with

40

unexpected things—crossroads, decision points—but we then have to respond, and if we do so in tune with His will, the outcome is creative.

Response implies choice: it is no more programmed reaction. Returning to the immense wisdom of Genesis, we can see the connection between the doctrine of Creation and that of Original Sin. Again, I shall have more to say of this later. For the moment, I will only register my appreciation of the doubts many Quakers have (and which I share) about calvinistic forms of the latter. I want to engage now in what I have found to be the current, enlightened approach to the problem of sin: an example, I think, of the way doctrine can develop reasonably without pretending to too much certainty, or betraying some of the most ancient truths about God.

At the heart of it lies a concept which may seem to deny the traditional view of God as almighty, omnipotent, able to work any miracle He pleases: the concept of the suffering of God, of God's weakness. Wherever I went among thinking churchmen, I kept hearing of this: you might almost call it fashionable. For example, I was told that the climax of the Church's year, the fortnight from Passion Sunday to Easter, is to be seen as the intense contemplation of God's weakness, suffering and vulnerability.

I find it hard to say whether this is a change in God or a change in our way of looking at Him. If it began as the former, the latter would have to follow in any case. As I absorb it, I find myself increasingly convinced that it is an aspect of Him which has always been there, but which is now turned squarely towards us.

It seems to me that unless we can come to terms with God's weakness the Christian faith is in vain. Unless we can make sense of it we cannot meet the first demand of the secular world, to show that God even exists. I say *show,* not *prove,* because anyone who expects the existence of God to be demonstrated by logic or measurement is playing at the wrong table from the start. If it were possible to prove God logically, we would all have to become His slaves, and that is not what a loving Father wants.

Those who know God (though none of us, even the most spiritual, has more than glimpsed His feet) know that God is indeed Love. We know that, fundamentally, the Universe is on our side: that it is permeated by a spirit that wills us to work with it, not against it, and a spirit that cares deeply and personally about us. I say that it grieves deeply and personally when we reject that will, that caring. And I say, too, that this is the central feature of the Cross—the point at which God and Mankind do cross—where God becomes Man and says 'I am like this—I am like you—and like you I am weak and I suffer'.

We can hear again the mocking call of the secular world I thought your God was omnipotent! But if we look more closely at Creation, we can see that from the very first appearance of Mankind, God surrenders power and weakens Himself, with that selfsame weakness that leads to the Cross.

The story of the *choice* of Adam and Eve to disobey God and help themselves to the power of moral decision symbolises God's gift to us of Free Will. I am not suggesting that our will is totally free, in the sense that we might have no social, historical or genetic bias working upon us. But it is free enough for us to know what it is, and to be responsible for our actions. All our decisions could have been made for us: we could have been programmed to do nothing but the best, to be nothing but God's puppets. He could have made us so entirely obedient to His will that we never conflicted with one another, never took risks, never ran into any kind of danger. But if you reflect upon that you will find that it amounts to saying that God could have made us not to be men and women at all. And He could have made us so completely aware of His will that—while we might have feared Him—we could never have loved Him of our own free choice. But Love, to be Love, cannot be coerced. It must be freely given. And that has to bring with it the freedom to withhold, to reject.

God wills our welfare; so His will is Love. Sin is the rejection of that loving will or, in the first place, the refusal even to listen for it. There is something nonsensical about such a refusal: how can any sensible person refuse what is the highest good? But time and again we find that sin does *not* make sense—in retrospect. Freedom, however, has to include the freedom to choose nonsense, to go against our own best interests by asserting that we know better than God and can do without Him.

God, then, has weakened Himself by giving us—like Adam and Eve—the freedom to reject Him. He is powerless if we choose to do so. For, as I have said, He can only be active in human affairs with our cooperation, with the concurrence of our love and His. We know very well, from our own experience, that love which is not recognised, responded to and returned is love incomplete and frustrated.

God has weakened Himself by constructing not an arbitrary Universe which He manipulates at whim, but a Universe of natural laws which He Himself must observe. A Universe of miraculous interventions would be a Universe of chaos, in which any freedom of choice on our part would be pointless. So God, too, loving His children, must suffer at the sight not only of the man-made disasters we bring upon ourselves but those natural disasters which, given the systems of the Universe, cannot but happen. As God suffers He longs, I am sure, that we would learn to understand those systems better and live with them more wisely.

It remains very hard for the non-believer to accept this line of argument. He still cannot accept that a loving God would allow a baby to fall into the fire, a peasant family to be crushed in an earthquake, a young mother to die in agony of cancer. It is a temptation to complain that anyone ever dies of anything, for the time is seldom ripe and pain is seldom absent altogether. I am not pretending that Christians can explain it all away in words: if there is a God, most of His ways must be far beyond us—but not all, for we believe that in revelation God goes out of His way to express Himself in terms that we can understand. I do not believe that God sets up disasters and contrives setbacks deliberately, in order to test us. But I do believe that out of every setback we can hear God demanding a creative response. In a world without suffering, we would grow no souls. Total bliss would be total oblivion.

So it happened that He whom the churches call God's own Son—the ultimate sign of God's love for us—was despised and rejected of man and nailed upon the Cross to be tortured to death, by Man's free will. And God was so weak that, His love being rejected, He could do nothing but hang there saying 'I am like this—I am like you'. He could do nothing but forgive, which is love, a form of love undeserved by those upon whom forgiveness is bestowed. Recognised, accepted and returned, it then becomes the mightiest power in the Universe: comforting, healing, pacifying and resurrecting. For no Christian can ever think of Crucifixion without immediately passing on to Resurrection. But first comes the weakness of God, and then His power—if we will grant it Him. For we, Mankind, stand between God and His power to be active through us. It is not our power, but His; yet we have the free will to frustrate it. And this, as Fox would say, I know experimentally.

So far, I have explored a tiny handful of some of the doctrinal insights that I found among the churches during my theological pilgimage: Creation, Sin, a spot of Revelation and Redemption. Some of them may have surprised you—surely the churches are not as broadminded as that? you may query—but I could cite eminent authority for all of them. I find them reasonable; they make sense in terms of my own experience; and I find it reasonable that they are, to a degree, uncertain. They are not completely watertight. They *could* be sunk. They do not explain everything, and I should be suspicious of them if they claimed to do so; for a God explained is a God limited, and so the wrong God. Let me repeat that I do not value doctrine for itself, but as a tool with which to work. It is the insight it produces that matters, not the doctrine *per se*. By insight, I mean that leap of understanding which confronts us with a glimpse of truth and leaves us knowing that we have glimpsed the will of God.

It would be very odd if, after some two thousand years of straining for such glimpses, the churches had not managed to encapsulate some of them in their doctrines. Friends certainly have in their ministry—spoken, written and acted—but what they have not attempted to do (or not much) is to set out a code of orthodoxy, of right teaching, let alone of right ritual. We advise and query and share our experience, but we do not really teach. We prefer to set people on the path of silence and encourage them to make their own discoveries there, unprejudiced by doctrine.

I am sure we are right in this, though I do not really believe that we can be or should be as independent of the rest of Christendom as we like to pretend. I have touched on this already, and I would only add now that it seems to me our openness to 'new light, from whatever quarter it may arise' should exclude—nor does Query 12 suggest that it should—the ancient lights of the historic churches.

What have they to tell us today about the Scriptures, about Salvation, about Incarnation, Authority, the Nature of Jesus and the Sacraments? Those, at any rate, are the doctrines I propose to touch upon in the remainder of this lecture.

Authority, of course, is a word to make any Quaker shudder; and quite right, too, if it means bringing pressure to bear on people to confess what they do not conscientiously and 'experimentally' believe. To your surprise, perhaps, you will find any Catholic priest agrees with you and will affirm the primacy of conscience—though he will add that it must be an 'informed' conscience, fully aware of what is involved. Equally you will find it quite impossible to get a Catholic priest to consign you to Hell. Such a destination is reserved for those who have fully understood the essential teaching of the Church and wilfully rejected it without repentance. Who is to say how fully, how wilfully, whether there may not have been inner repentance at the last? God alone, I was told. I have no doubt that there are still 'good Catholics' who are taught to believe everything the Church teaches, and who pride themselves on it; but there is plenty of evidence that the great majority are discreetly more selective. You may think that dishonest or a disservice to Truth; but it also reveals a certain tact and sense of basic solidarity. People are reluctant to upset their priests and cause a scandal by insisting upon the scrapping of doctrines in which the Church has invested so much effort. Authority, in the punitive sense, holds very few terrors today. When it comes to matters like divorce and birth-control, Catholics please themselves and behave much like anyone else.

But in a deeper sense, Authority means the ultimate guarantee of Truth: the promise that the teachings of a church are *authoritative* and authentic; and traditionally there are two sources of this, Scripture and Tradition.

To the Catholic Church (and remember, the Church of England claims also to be Catholic) tradition is assured by the Apostolic Succession, a literal handing down from the apostles. It is easy enough to dismiss that, both on the grounds of historical dubiousness and because of the unlikelihood that a twentieth-century bishop and a first-century apostle would understand the same words in the same way, even supposing they shared the same words. Terms like 'the resurrection of the body', 'the real presence', 'maker of heaven and earth' do not have the same resonances for us that they had even three hundred years ago, and they must have been different again a thousand years before that.

But that *something* is handed down cannot be denied. Quakers, with their much shorter history, are surely aware of being the heirs in more than name to Fox and his Valiant Sixty. They suffered, and somehow they survived. That survival, the fact that there was and apparently still is something to pass on gives whatever-it-is an authenticity that seems more than human. Confronted by the visible effects of such power, who are we to brush it aside?

I must confess that I get a little weary of those whose arguments against the Church in general (and the Roman Catholic Church in particular) consist of a catalogue of scandals and persecutions, of dissenters burnt at the stake or torn upon the rack, of popes debauching themselves in the Vatican upon the proceeds of their indulgent salesmen, of empires colonised in the name of Jesus and truth suppressed in the name of orthodoxy. Such catalogues invariably end by blaming the Pope for not excommunicating the IRA—though what good that would do among a pack of godless murderers who have already excommunicated themselves, I have never been able to fathom.

The point is, however, that the Roman Church's claim to right doctrine does not seem to have made it, or its leaders and followers, morally any better. Its authority, we are told, has been either corrupt or futile.

Let me hastily add that it is hardly fair to limit these charges to Rome. Protestant princes have slaughtered as ruthlessly as Catholics, Anglican prelates have wallowed in considerable luxury, and Protestant Elizabeth made as many martyrs as her Catholic sister Mary. Friends need only consult their own history to find the record of Puritan and Anglican intolerance. Nor have we always been models of tolerance ourselves.

What this tells me is that doctrine actually has very little to do with making people good. It is, as I have said, a desperate attempt to package up and pass on some aspect of the truth about God. But, like everything in the Christian faith, it is not a magic spell. It may inform, but it does not transform. The only thing that does that is grace, which is nothing else than the free and unmerited gift of God's love, a gift to which we are free to shut our doors or even reject it. It is, alas, perfectly possible for prelate, prince or presbyter to have a quiverful of right doctrines and yet be utterly lacking in grace.

What use, then is it to claim authority for one's doctrines? First, it gives us a certain solidarity with holy people of the past and enables us to enter into their insights. There is a certain arrogance in pretending that no generation till ours had a valid religious experience. Next, by availing ourselves of that insight and experience and accepting—if only provisionally—its formulations we gain access to its language: we can use it *as if* it were true. This may seem a hypocritical way to seek God, but in fact it is a humble one. If we insist upon complete certainty that a formulation is true we shall make no progress at all, for it is God we are talking about and we cannot possibly encompass

Him or any part of Him with human language. The best we can do is to take up some instrument forged by people we have reason to trust and use it *as if* it were reliable, up to the point where it ceases to be so. At that point we have to think again, perhaps even ask ourselves whether we need to go any further or whether the provisional will, in fact, do.

There is in the Quaker tradition, however, a strong and healthy tendency to leap over this kind of argument by maintaining that it is precisely the obsession with using forms of words that has bogged the churches down. As our late, great Friend George Gorman used to say: 'Friends have always felt that what matters is how you follow Jesus, and not theories about Him and His divinity. There is a great scepticism in the Society about things we cannot *know*.[11]

Rightly so, I think. We are practical mystics rather than impractical theologians. We have always been better at doing our faith than at saying it, better at meeting God than at describing Him afterwards; and there must be some here (or perhaps they have left by now) who regard this lecture as a complete waste of time. For when you have met God, it seems to matter very little whether He was wearing a blue tie or a green one and whether He had a long white beard or was, in fact, Our Mother.

I have deliberately gone too far there. Doctrine is not about anything so trivial. Nor is it true that all believers—or even all Friends—are content with direct apprehensions of the divine. For one thing, not everybody has such apprehensions; and I would resist the claim of some 'born again' Christians that unless you have been personally struck down on the Damascus Road you are not really a Christian at all. Faith, as I have said, is heart and guts as well as head: pure reason will bring nobody to the Kingdom of Heaven. But I know plenty of good Christians, including Quakers, who have laboured their way to their faith, step by step, without ever making a tremendous leap

49

into the dark. Their religious life does not lack its moments of contemplation and awe, but it also includes long passages of argument—with themselves, with other people, with books. That is simply the way many of us are, or have been brought up to be, and we cannot pursue our interior life without some attempt at formulations, some resort to language.

Naturally enough, we look to Scripture for guidance. For if anything has authority, it is surely the Bible. Even Fox would have been lost without it, for it gave him the language and concepts with which to communicate his own experience.

The heaviest barrage of criticism fired against the *Priestland's Progress* series came from fundamentalist evangelicals who roared: 'Stop raising doubts! It is all perfectly simple, and it is all in the Bible!' I could only tell them that, so far as I could see, it was very far from simple and the Bible contained either too much or too little. It requires enormous scholarship to figure out whether—for example—Jesus really did think the end of the world was approaching, let alone to understand the prophetic books of the Old Testament. There is scarcely a heresy that cannot claim to be justified by scripture. And yet the New Testament is maddeningly silent or obscure about events after the Resurrection, and the early history of the Church. What did St Peter get up to after the end of Acts? Was he ever really in Rome at all?

At this point, the Church steps in with its authority and its traditions. Admittedly we have nothing better, but it would be very naive to accept tradition as if it were objective history. It is equally naive to regard the Bible in the same way, for the Bible is actually the creation of the Church—it, too, is tradition and we cannot separate Bible and Church. But that means that every book in the New Testament must be regarded as a doctrinal treatise, not a work of record alone. Again, enormous scholarship is needed to understand it aright. Being no scholar

50

myself, I find two maxims helpful:

(1) A text means what its author meant it to mean.

(2) What must its significance be for us now, if an author writing in the xth century wrote as he did then?

These maxims hardly simplify matters, I admit. But they make two points, adverse to fundamentalists, which were underlined by all the serious scholars I spoke with. (1) emphasises that the primary meaning of a text is governed by its original circumstances, not by ours. (2) emphasises that if it has any meaning for us, that must take account of the change in circumstances, including language, culture and modes of thought. Fox would have said that the scriptures themselves were lifeless unless they were recreated by the Spirit within the heart of the reader; and it seems to me that the remarkable endurance of the Bible—what makes it 'the Word of God'—is that there was so much of the Spirit in its writing that it constantly evokes the Spirit in its reading. But in every age, according to human circumstances, it is different things that are drawn up from the depths of scripture to be reborn. Jesus Himself treated it selectively. And (goodness knows!) so do the fundamentalists. But there is a world of difference between allowing life to play freely upon the Bible—illuminating a passage here and a passage there—and seeking to impose the Bible flatly upon life. All scripture has had its authority, its authenticity, for the particular circumstances in which it was written, and some of those circumstances abide permanently in the human condition. But others change drastically, and to ignore that is, in fact, to ignore the creative activity of God.

7

There are few questions of faith that embarrass people more than the doctrine of the Incarnation—the divinity of Christ. Was He not only *the* Son of God (few churches permit us to say *a* Son of God), but God himself? Quakers often decline to play this particular game, regarding it as the thin end of that credal wedge that has split up Christendom into so many splinters. But it is crucial to the Christian tradition and many Friends do engage with it to the extent of saying either 'Yes, Jesus was uniquely divine' or 'No, He was just a very good man indeed.' I suppose there must be some who would reply agnostically 'I have no means of knowing either way': but in my book, that goes down as a No. To suggest that Jesus *might* have been divine but left the case not proven seems to me to be taking a very strange view of God. Either the demonstration is there or it is not.

Many nominal Christians belong to the 'Jesus was a very good man' brigade, and some would go so far as to add '— probably the best there has ever been', though I fancy they would find it difficult to explain just why he was the best. But according to the doctrine of the mainstream churches, such people are not really Christians at all. According to such doctrines (maintained by George Fox, too, in his own language) Jesus was not just a teacher, preacher, healer and prophet, and a fine example to all of us of ethical living: He was God's only begotten Son who takes away the sins of the world, and thus (since God is One and Indivisible) He was God. If you are merely a follower and admirer of Jesus, say the churches, you have missed the point; your faith is incomplete; you have to believe, know and feel that He was and still is God.

The 'still is' is very important and should raise little difficulty for Friends. Fox found that 'there *is* one, even Christ Jesus, that can speak to thy condition'—not that there used to be one, and throughout his teaching the Light is Christ, not the personal private conscience. Fox is not talking about a passive example of goodness, either, but of an active agent against chaos and sin.

Far be it from me to establish a doctrine of Foxian Infallibility. There is no such thing. I know plenty of Friends who cannot, in good conscience, acknowledge the unique divinity of Christ. I know some who find there are two or more who also speak to their condition—the Buddha, Krishna of the Gita. My only intention here is to suggest at least one way in which the Incarnation might be seen to make sense as a useful doctrine for us also.

The notion that God should have taken flesh in the shape of a first century Galilean carpenter's son immediately raises the Scandal of Particularity: the stumbling-block, that is, of the question 'Why this particular person, place and time rather than any other, or several others?' Apart from anything else, it seems unfair on those who have missed the Christian bus, through no fault of their own, by being at the wrong place or in the wrong time.

One cannot begin to answer this without first observing that if there was to be an Incarnation, it was bound to be particular. The choice of time, place and circumstances was (if God will excuse my patronising Him) rather clever. What would not have been clever is a series of Incarnations, scattered about the globe, each bound to develop into a competitive regional cult. Things are bad enough as they are.

We need not, I think, take too seriously the objection that particularity implies the damnation of all non-Christians. I do not see that Jesus believed any such thing, and today damnation itself is a notion that stands condemned. All that seems to be left of Hell (and it is bad enough) is the wilful rejection, at the last, of the love of God. It is something personal between God and the individual soul, for which no certificate can be issued by anyone here on earth. Nor can time—whether B.C. or A.D.—be of any relevance at the last assize. It is not a serious proposition among theologians today that Thomas More will enjoy a higher place in Heaven than Socrates, or, for that matter, that doors will be open to St Francis that will be closed to Guru Nanak of the Sikhs.

But surely doctrine says otherwise? 'I am the way, the truth and the life. No man comes to the Father except by Me.' At first sight this is the most exclusive and pitiless of Christ's sayings, and it is often cited to me by conservative evengelicals as an example of His supreme authority. 'It sounds ungenerous, I know,' said one, 'But He could not, on the authority given Him by His Father, have said otherwise.'

One might dodge round the problem by denying that Jesus used any such words. They appear only in *John,* and *John* may be either the most authentic or the least authentic of the gospels. However, the weeding out of inconvenient texts is a slippery slope and I am inclined, myself, to accept that Jesus did use those words.

The maxims of interpretation which I mentioned earlier urge us to begin by recalling the circumstances in which they were first employed. Jesus was warning his disciples against contaminating his teachings with those of rival teachers of that time. But He cannot possibly have been addressing himself to the Hindus, Chinese and North American Indians of any time. And what can His words mean to us today, if He spoke as He did then? Do they mean that Quakers are wrong to look for new light, wherever it may come from?

I am not one of those who believes that 'one religion is as good as another—they are basically all the same'. This is partly because it simply is not true—some religions are radically different in purpose from others; partly because I have no idea how one could judge 'as good as': greater amounts of happiness or truth produced, larger numbers of souls saved? It is a fairly futile argument, in any case, since religion is inevitably affected by cultural surroundings, and in the end things simply are as they are. Most Muslims are Muslim because they were born in the Middle East, not because they made a free choice. It happens that there is a greater freedom of religious choice today than there has ever been; and we are all of us free to admire the ingenuity with which God has found ways of speaking to many different cultures in the ways appropriate to them. Some of those ways may speak to us, too, and I see no harm in responding to them.

But religion seeks to make sense of the circumstances in which we are. Being involves thinking, working, breeding, dying and every activity in between. In the circumstances of our own Western culture, I cannot see anything to commend any serious departure from the Christian faith; no point, for example, in Britain converting to Hinduism or Islam. I can actually find as much transcendental meditation as I need in Mother Julian and *The Cloud of Unknowing,* and this helps me to find rewards in the oriental religions. The trouble is, I find them curiously static. Because I do not share their modes of thinking and living and do not instinctively know how to use their doctrinal tools, I find myself just visiting the oriental faiths rather than taking up residence in them.

One great advantage of Christianity—as the growing churches of the Third World are discovering—is that it is, despite its doctrines, a progressive and developing religion. It has a far greater potential for adaptation to local conditions and far greater freedom of theology than any of its sister faiths. You hear complaints about this from some Christian quarters—that there is not enough certainty and stability, far too much heterodoxy and experiment—but to say that doctrine has stifled enquiry and discouraged the extension of the faith does not stand up to the facts. On the face of it, it is vastly improbable that a faith which was born in Palestine and received its basic formulation in Asia Minor would spread to Ireland and Ethiopia and eventually find enthusiastic support in Malabar and Mexico, but that is the case. The Society of Friends has spread, too, without a comparable framework: but not, we must admit, to the same extent. And if we are honest, we must admit that we would be nowhere at all without the foundations laid by the churches.

Few of us have come to the Father except by Christ, and we would know little if anything of Christ but for the churches and the systems they have devised for packaging and transmitting their information about Him. But can *no* man approach God except by the Christian way? Surely, any of us must say that if the humble Bengali on the banks of the Ganges cannot get to Heaven unless he becomes a Baptist—or a Catholic—or an Anglican—then God is not the God we know or would want to know. And I do not think that is what Christ was saying. I believe He was saying 'The way, the truth and the life are all what I stand for. Anyone who seeks them sincerely is on his way to my Father.'

Am I guilty of watering down the words of the gospel, to make them easier? But the Church has always been aware of the problem of the virtuous pagan or Jew. Certainly St Paul was. And what must the truth be now—now that the gospel has been preached for almost two thousand years—if, in a much narrower world, Christ insisted that there was no alternative to His way, His life? I think the truth is that He was right, but in a much broader sense than He or His disciples could have understood then.

I am supposed to be grappling with the Doctrine of

57

Incarnation, which is a very particular doctrine, and all I have done is generalise. Quakers believe that there is an element of God in everyone, and that good occurs when the God within responds to the God without. But classically it was never just God, it was Christ; for Christ is God with a human face, the God who is also man. Because He is man, He suffers and dies like man. Because He is God, He cannot die but rises again and lives on in all of us. But why Christ—Jesus of Nazareth, son of Joseph the carpenter? Why not simply the Holy Spirit? Because the essence of the human condition is its particularity. We are all of us unique individuals in a particular place and time, and God would not have been fully human if He, too, had not been once-for-all in the same way. There is a paradox here, because He also is and always has been present in everyone. But we could not recognise this fully without the sacramental sign of the historical Jesus.

Sacramental is, of course, a suspect word among Friends, which is a pity. No, I am not proposing that we indulge in Eucharists or sprinklings: if you fancy them occasionally, they are easy enough to get elsewhere. But many of us fail to understand what the others are up to and fail also to grasp how essentially sacramental all religious life really is. We tend to be put off by the Catholic view that sacraments have to be mediated to the laity by the Church, and, incidentally, that the mediator has to be an ordained male. There are some interesting signs that this view is crumbling before the consensus of the faithful, like Catholic teaching on contraception. For a long time, for example, it has been accepted that anyone *can* baptise. Marriage, as a sacrament, is a relatively late development, and for better or worse is being dispensed with increasingly. The celibate male-only priesthood will not survive this century; and increasing numbers of house-church Christians are not only sharing communion interdenominationally, but doing it without an ordained minister.

The real essence of a sacrament is that it is a visible sign of grace. Grace is not only the love of God for man—free and regardless of our merit: it is our response to that love. It is a two-way affair. That is how the sacraments of the Church have become acts of worship: a sign of love is received from God, and a sign is returned to Him.

Friends, who rightly refuse to distinguish between life and religious life, should be well accustomed to receiving the sacraments of friendship, truth, beauty, integrity in their daily lives (and very often they are mediated to us by others). They may also be able to see, in the person of Christ, a sacrament of unequalled power, a sign of unmerited love that demands love in response and thus becomes in itself an act of worship. It seems to me that it is this quality of being worshipped, of having been worshipped, of worshipfulness that endows Christ with much of his divinity. It is almost as if Jesus was God because we say so. Once, I found myself writing 'If Jesus was not God—He is now'. In the same mysterious way, it also occurred to me that in Jesus God was saying 'I am like *this*. Indeed, I am so like this that as far as you will ever know I *am* this.'

I realise that there are many who cannot say 'I make Christ God', and others who cannot agree that my myth-making accords with the creeds. It has been put to me that the notion of Jesus somehow *becoming* god is not at all what the Incarnation is about. Nor have I given any clue so far as to how the death of Jesus on the Cross might 'take away our sins'.

To cover that adequately would double the length of this lecture. But if Jesus was not in some sense God, so that His suffering and death were a sign to us of how God absorbs human evil and does not defend Himself but returns to comfort His betrayers, then it is hard to see how He could be of more than literary interest to us at all. Equally, if He was not also

59

man, His suffering and death would have been a divine stunt in poor taste. The doctrine of Incarnation insists that He was both, that He still is both, and that He remains lovingly and painfully involved in our lives and deaths.

To what end? Church doctrine answers 'Our salvation', and I have had the gravest struggles with this for two reasons: first, because like many Friends I believe the Church has taken an unduly oppressive view of our need for salvation; second, because at this point the Church breaks up into many churches, each with its own pet doctrine.

There is an apparent contradiction, however, between the basic assumption of almost all the churches about Original Sin and Fox's own experience of going up into Paradise and being freed from it. It is true that Fox acknowledged it was Christ who had freed him. Nevertheless, he shocked the ministers of his day by refusing to join them in 'roaring up for sin' (as he put it), and I have found Friends to this day relatively uninterested in—or at least, relatively unoppressed by—human wickedness. Dear George Gorman used to say 'We tend to start from the opposite of Original Sin.' He also told me he spent a great deal of his time trying to 'de-guilt' people who had been torn and smashed by their sense of sin; and I know from personal experience precisely what he meant.

There is obviously something of the child-parent relationship in all this. Our relationship with our parents points us upwards so that when we achieve maturity we seek a similar relationship with the Father of all of us. And just as we fear that our infant naughtiness will lose us the love of our earthly parents (without which we cannot survive), so we come to fear that our spiritual offences will render us utterly repulsive to God, whom we are told constantly we should love, even though He apparently has the power to annihilate us.

I still meet clergy who insist that all of us, even the most

60

evidently virtuous, are so totally depraved that we deserve that annihilation, and would indeed receive it at the hands of a just God were it not for the fact that Christ has 'paid the price for our sins—undergone the punishment in our place—sacrificed Himself for the world'. To me, that proposes a God who is unspeakably barbarous, but I am told that is because I am presuming to Judge Him in human terms. My own intuition is that God judges *us* in human terms, for after all He is responsible for our humanity and would be condemning His own work if He did otherwise. I suspect the savage view of God derived from an age when relatively little was understood of natural cause and effect, and a great many events must have seemed either miracles or divine punishments. To this day people wonder why God destroys innocent babies in earth-quakes, instead of expecting earthquakes to occur in earth-quake zones and building accordingly.

Fortunately there is a more merciful doctrine of sin and salvation, which I now find to be in the ascendent. It sees us not as fallen and depraved, but as striving (or not, as the case may be) towards a height where we have never been before but to which we are called by God. His will for us is, in fact, the pattern of our true nature, and to follow it is to be true to our humanity. The difficulty is that we have been given the free will to think we know better—a supreme gift of the loving Father, without which we would be mere puppets, not worth having and not worth being either.

Where, then, is Christ's salvation? How could his death on the Cross be of any help to us? For if the theology I have outlined is valid, it would seem that we could hardly be to blame for failing to do better than we do. If blame lay anywhere, it would lie with God for demanding the impossible of us, and for giving us too little help. And do we need salvation at all? Why can we not approach our end, in good conscience, claiming to have done our best in the circumstances?

Superficially this attitude is very appealing, but I think any Friend who has cultivated the discipline of silent contemplation will have already encountered the objections to it. Surely we know that the blame does *not* lie with God; that He has constantly been prompting us towards the right path which we have not followed. I would reject the abject confession that 'there is no health in us', but despite the health that is in us we continue to choose disorder. However, the doctrine I find in the New Testament is not that we are therefore damned, but that if we repent—if we recognise that disorder is of our own choosing—we are not alienated from God but are instantly forgiven, restored to contact with Him and set back in line with our proper nature. Jesus said constantly to people 'Your sins are forgiven'. He did not tell them their sins would be forgiven if they uttered certain words or performed certain rituals. They were forgiven all the time—God recognised the circumstances of sin—if only they would acknowledge their need of forgiveness, reach out and take it.

But again, what has the Cross to do with this? As I read the doctrines of the Church, we cannot break Christ up into optional fragments: we cannot take His life apart from His death apart from His resurrection. The doctrine of the Trinity (which I had hoped to spare you) may seem an unnecessary complication to us today, but it arose because the early Church found it absolutely necessary to explain the totality of its experience. God the Father had always been familiar to the Jews. His disciples were convinced that Jesus was His Incarnation, His Son upon earth. Even after his departure, He was still in touch with them through the Holy Spirit. Each was distinct, yet all were from the same source. Just so, the death of Christ was an inevitable part of His life, and that life was a sign, a showing of the Way God Is: living like us, suffering and dying like us under conditions of deep injustice, the more unjust because His life had been one of uncompromised love and well-doing. Yet His death brought no revenge, but forgiveness. It led not to the extinction of his teaching, but His resurrection and triumph.

One stream of theology has sought to interpret this in terms of a superhuman change in the moral chemistry of the universe. The blood of Christ has somehow neutralised the corrosive acid of Adam's original sin, making it possible for a Supreme God who was until then willing but unable to be reconciled with man to accept man back in His bosom.

Even if we tinker with time, arguing that Christ's sacrifice was from the beginning, it seems to me that this kind of doctrine postulates a God who plays with us needlessly. If I am right in believing (as the story of Adam's Fall asserts) that the essence of sin is our own free will, then the very existence of God—or rather, the recognition that He exists—depends upon human free will. God does not exist unless we want Him to exist, and if we do not want Him, He becomes powerless.

In order to explain this perhaps shocking statement it is necessary to use words paradoxically. Believing, as I do, that God does exist I also believe that even if we were to make Him vanish in this way He would still exist. He does not depend upon our recognition of Him, any more than an undiscovered galaxy does, or Gravity did before Newton put it on paper. I do not believe that God is mere wish-fulfilment, the construction of our desires. I can see how man might desire a divine Father-figure, and how he might send up smoke signals to Heaven appealing to such a figure. But I do not think religion would have developed and survived if there had been no response to such signals. I would say God initiated the exchange Himself, even if His signals were not recognised for what they were.

For all I know, it is not impossible that some 'salvation signal', a sign of how God was and how man could be reconciled with Him through suffering, forgiveness and resurrection, was sent to us before Jesus. It is not impossible that there were garbled or unrecognised signals, signals that were incomplete because the atmospheric conditions were not favourable to reception. It may be that this was a signal God had always been sending to us, but that for the first time, in Christ, it was received in its true form; picked up on a human receiver accurately tuned in to the divine wavelength. I must apologise if I seem to be exploiting a convenient modern metaphor, but it does present me with a way of understanding what the doctrine of unique salvation is trying to say. By hanging between God and man, eternal life and inevitable death, Jesus saves us from the breakdown of communications: and in that exchange, we have almost as great a part to play as God Himself. God recognises Himself in Christ, and we recognise ourselves.

It is, of course, a metaphor and therefore an uncertainty; though not, I hope, an unreasonable one. To me it makes enough sense for me to be able to go on with the business of exploring God, and that is what doctrine has always sought to do. It is a mistake to regard it today as a kind of legislation or as a test of membership of the Christian community. I do not deny that there are groups within the churches who think otherwise, insisting that unless you firmly and truly believe in Justification by Faith or Transubstantiation you are not a Christian at all. They are precisely the people whom Quakers have always opposed, the shutters out rather than inviters in. I must report that during my own wandering through the Christian family I found such exclusiveness very much out of fashion. Education and enquiry have made it impossible for the clergy to maintain that doctrine is really final. There is no way in which they can threaten the doubter with Hell fire. Doctrine is now revealed for what it always was, an alternative to silence, a package of provisional information, a tool to work with for those who need to work with words.

I have always suspected that one characteristic of the natural Friend is that he is not an instinctively wordy person. That may be an odd thing to say in a Society noted, if not notorious, for its committees and its epistles. But we have always believed in deeds rather than words, our origins were among working people rather than intellectuals, and our strength is in the contemplative rather than intellectual life. 'This' Fox knew experimentally, not intellectually.

And yet we have a large number of intellectuals among us. As I have already said, we must admit that we owe a great deal to what we have brought from other churches. I cannot conceive that we would ever wish to merge with them institutionally. But I do think we need to stay in touch with them, for our sake, for their sake, and for the sake of the truth. Reasonableness, in the sense of open-mindedness, is a paramount Quaker virtue. Uncertainty, in the sense of not pretending to know everything, runs alongside it. Reasonable uncertainty is now the outstanding characteristic of doctrinal thinking in Britain. I have found it as widespread among Roman Catholics as among the broad Church of England, the Methodists and the United Reformed. We should not be surprised that they will not entirely let go of doctrine, for it provides both an intellectual discipline against which the speculator must prove his merits, and a route back to the treasurehouse of the Christian past. Doctrine, despite its dialects, remains a common language among our fellow believers. It is no longer to be seen as a set of chains but as a set of ropes with which to climb the summitless mountain ahead.

REFERENCES

[1] *Advices and Queries*. London Yearly Meeting, 1964

[2] Gerald Priestland, *Priestland's Progress*. BBC Publications, 1981, or on cassettes from Christian Broadcast Training, 3 Bury Road, Newmarket CB8 7BS. Also summarised in *The Listener*

[3] George Fox, *Journal* ed. John Nickalls. London Yearly Meeting, 1952, rptd. 1975, p. 11

[4] Janet Scott, *What canst thou say? Towards a Quaker theology* (Swarthmore Lecture, 1980). London: Quaker Home Service, 1980

[5] John Macmurray, *The search for reality in religion* (Swarthmore Lecture, 1965). London: Quaker Home Service, 1965, rptd. 1969

[6] *Advices and Queries,* op. cit

[7] *Christian Faith and Practice in the experience of the Society of Friends*. London Yearly Meeting, 1960

[8] Yorkshire Quarterly Meeting's Memorandum on the Book of Discipline, section V: The Scriptures. In Yearly Meeting Proceedings. 1919. Quoted from *Christian Faith and Practice,* § 202

[9] *Advices and Queries,* op. cit

[10] Michael P. Hornsby-Smith and Raymond M. Lee, *Roman Catholic Opinion: final report*. Department of Sociology, University of Surrey, 1979.

[11] See similarly, *Introducing Quakers* by George H. Gorman. London: Quaker Home Service, 1969, 5th rpt. 1980, p. 18.

The books listed above are obtainable from the FRIENDS BOOK CENTRE, FRIENDS HOUSE, EUSTON ROAD, LONDON NW1 2BJ. A full list of Quaker literature will be sent on request.